Illustrated Landmark for Children:

The Eiffel Tower

A Marvel of Engineering and Beauty

Visit our author page for more books:
Amazon.com/author/88

By Nicole Damon

Introduction: The Marvelous Eiffel Tower

Welcome, young adventurers! Are you ready to embark on a journey to one of the most famous landmarks in the world? Let's explore the magnificent Eiffel Tower, a towering symbol of beauty and ingenuity that stands proudly in the heart of Paris, France.

Imagine a gigantic iron structure, as tall as an 81-story building, reaching up to touch the sky. That's the Eiffel Tower! It's not just any tower; it's a masterpiece of engineering that has captivated the hearts of people from all around the globe.

But why is the Eiffel Tower so special? Well, when it was completed in 1889, it was the tallest man-made structure in the world. It was built for the World's Fair, a big event where countries show off their most impressive inventions and creations.

The tower is named after a very smart engineer, Gustave Eiffel, who had a big dream. He and his company worked hard to design and build this amazing tower. Gustave Eiffel put his name on it, just like an artist signs a painting, to show that he was proud of this incredible creation. So, whenever you hear the name "Eiffel Tower," you can think of Gustave Eiffel and his amazing dream that came to life!

The Eiffel Tower isn't just famous for its height; it's also a symbol of Paris, the city of love and light. It's like a beacon, shining bright and welcoming visitors to explore its beauty and the rich history of France. Over the years, it has become a beloved icon, representing the creativity and spirit of the French people.

A Dream in Iron

Once upon a time, in the beautiful city of Paris, there lived a brilliant engineer named Gustave Eiffel. Gustave was not just any engineer; he had a vision, a dream to build something that the world had never seen before. Little did he know that his dream would become one of the most famous landmarks in the world—the Eiffel Tower!

In the late 1800s, France was preparing for a grand event called the Exposition Universelle, or the World's Fair, to be held in 1889. This fair was a big deal because it was going to celebrate the 100th anniversary of the French Revolution, a time when the people of France fought for freedom and equality. The organizers of the fair wanted something spectacular to show off to the world, and that's where Gustave Eiffel came in.

Gustave had an idea for a tower made entirely of iron that would be the centerpiece of the fair. It would be so tall that it would reach the clouds, and people could go up and see Paris from above. The design was like a giant puzzle, with over 18,000 pieces of iron and 2.5 million rivets holding it all together!

But building the Eiffel Tower was not an easy task. Many people doubted that it could be done. They thought that a tower made of iron would be too heavy and would just collapse. Some even thought it would be an eyesore and ruin the beauty of Paris. Gustave Eiffel, however, was determined to prove them wrong.

The construction of the tower faced many challenges. It was like building a giant Lego structure, but with heavy iron beams and without the instructions! The workers had to climb high into the sky, with nothing but ropes to keep them safe. They worked through wind, rain, and cold, piecing together the tower bit by bit.

Despite all the difficulties, Gustave Eiffel's dream did not crumble. In just two years, the tower was completed, and it was even more magnificent than anyone had imagined. It stood tall and proud, a symbol of human ingenuity and perseverance.

The Eiffel Tower was the star of the 1889 World's Fair, and it quickly became a beloved landmark of Paris. Gustave Eiffel's dream in iron had become a reality, and it continues to inspire people from all over the world to this day. So, the next time you see a picture of the Eiffel Tower, remember the story of Gustave Eiffel and his incredible iron dream!

Building the Giant

Building the Eiffel Tower was like putting together a giant jigsaw puzzle, but with iron pieces and no picture to guide the builders! It was a huge challenge, but Gustave Eiffel and his team were ready to make history. First, let's talk about the materials. The tower is made almost entirely of iron—over 7,300 tons of it! That's heavier than a thousand elephants! The iron was formed into beams and girders, which are like the skeleton of the tower.

To build the tower, workers had to assemble these iron pieces just right. They used a technique called "riveting," which is like using metal pins to hold the pieces together. Imagine trying to hold two giant metal beams in place and then hammering a hot, glowing rivet through them to keep them together. That's what the workers did, over and over again, until all 18,038 pieces were securely fastened with 2.5 million rivets.

Now, building something as tall as the Eiffel Tower was no small feat. The workers had to climb up high, carrying heavy iron pieces and tools. They didn't have the modern safety equipment we have today, so it was a risky job. But they were determined and skilled, and they worked together like a well-oiled machine.

One of the most innovative techniques used in the construction was the use of hydraulic jacks. These are like big, powerful pumps that can lift heavy weights. As the tower grew taller, the jacks lifted the iron sections into place, like building a giant Lego tower, but with iron instead of plastic bricks!

The teamwork and dedication of the workers were incredible. They braved all kinds of weather, from scorching heat to freezing cold, and worked tirelessly to bring Gustave Eiffel's vision to life. It took two years, two months, and five days of hard work to complete the tower. That's pretty fast, considering they were building one of the tallest structures in the world!

When the tower was finally finished, it was a sight to behold. It stood tall and strong, a testament to the ingenuity and teamwork of all those who worked on it. The Eiffel Tower was not just a marvel of engineering; it was a symbol of what people can achieve when they work together with determination and skill.

The Tower Through Time

After the Eiffel Tower was completed in 1889, it was like a new star had appeared in the sky over Paris. But believe it or not, not everyone loved it at first. Some people thought it was too tall and strange-looking. They couldn't imagine how this giant iron tower could fit in with the beautiful, historic buildings of Paris. In fact, some famous artists and writers even signed a petition to have it taken down!

Despite the initial criticism, the Eiffel Tower quickly won the hearts of Parisians and visitors from around the world. It became the most popular attraction at the 1889 World's Fair, with millions of people coming to see it and ride the elevators to the top for a breathtaking view of Paris.

Over time, the Eiffel Tower has witnessed many important events in history. During World War I, it played a crucial role as a radio tower, helping to intercept enemy messages and coordinate French troops. Imagine the tower, once criticized for its appearance, becoming a hero in the war!

In World War II, when German forces occupied Paris, they actually hung a swastika flag from the top of the tower. But as a symbol of defiance, the French cut the elevator cables so the Germans had to climb the stairs if they wanted to reach the top. That's over 1,700 steps!

The Eiffel Tower has also been a place of celebration and joy. In 2000, it was adorned with sparkling lights to welcome the new millennium, turning it into a glittering beacon of hope for the future.

But the Eiffel Tower is not just a historical monument; it's also been a place of scientific discovery. Gustave Eiffel himself used the tower for experiments in meteorology, aerodynamics, and even radio broadcasting. The tower has been home to weather stations, antennas, and even a secret military bunker!

Today, the Eiffel Tower is more than just a symbol of Paris; it's a symbol of human creativity, resilience, and the spirit of adventure. It has stood the test of time, evolving from a controversial structure to a beloved icon, witnessing the unfolding story of Paris and the world. So, the next time you see the Eiffel Tower, remember the incredible journey it has been on and the many stories it has to tell.

A Closer Look

Come along, young explorers, as we take a virtual tour of the magnificent Eiffel Tower! With its three levels, incredible elevators, and breathtaking views, there's so much to discover.

First, let's start at the bottom and work our way up. The first level of the Eiffel Tower is like a welcoming entrance to this iron wonder. It's not just a place to stand and look up; it's a whole world of its own! There are shops, restaurants, and even a small museum where you can learn more about the tower's history. And if you're brave enough, you can walk on the glass floor and see the ground far below your feet!

Now, let's take one of the tower's famous elevators. These aren't just any elevators; they're specially designed to travel up the tower's slanted legs. As we ascend, you can see the iron lattice work getting closer, like a giant spider web made of metal.

We've reached the second level, and wow, what a view! From here, you can see the beautiful River Seine, the grand Louvre Museum, and the majestic Notre Dame Cathedral. There's even a restaurant here where you can enjoy a meal with a view like no other.

Ready to go even higher? Let's take another elevator ride up to the third and final level. This is the highest public observation deck in the European Union, at a dizzying height of about 276 meters (905 feet) above the ground. The view from up here is simply breathtaking. You can see the whole city of Paris spread out beneath you, with its charming streets, elegant bridges, and famous landmarks.

But the Eiffel Tower isn't just famous for its height and views. Have you ever seen it sparkle at night? Every evening, the tower is illuminated with 20,000 golden lights that make it glow like a jewel. And for five minutes every hour on the hour, it puts on a dazzling light show, with the lights twinkling and dancing in the night. This magical display is not just for show; it's a way of celebrating the beauty and spirit of Paris, the City of Light.

The Eiffel Tower Today

Today, the Eiffel Tower stands tall and proud as a symbol of Paris and France. It's not just a piece of history; it's a living, breathing part of the city that continues to awe and inspire.

A Tourist's Dream:

Every year, millions of visitors from all around the world come to see the Eiffel Tower. Visitors from all over the world step into the tower's elevators, which whisk them up to the very top. Once there, they pull out their cameras and snap photos to capture the moment.

They gaze out in wonder at the stunning views of Paris spread out below them, with its winding streets, beautiful buildings, and famous landmarks like the River Seine and Notre Dame Cathedral. It's a moment they'll remember forever! The tower is especially popular at night when it lights up the sky with its golden glow and sparkling light show.

A Symbol of Love:

The Eiffel Tower is also known as a symbol of love. Couples come to the tower to take romantic walks, propose marriage, or simply enjoy the beautiful views together. It's no wonder that Paris is called the City of Love!

A Platform for Events:

The Eiffel Tower is not just for sightseeing; it's also used for special events and celebrations. From New Year's Eve fireworks to Bastille Day light shows, the tower is a centerpiece for many of Paris's biggest festivities.

Renovations and Upgrades:

To keep the Eiffel Tower looking its best, it undergoes regular renovations and upgrades. In recent years, the tower has seen improvements to its elevators, security systems, and visitor facilities. The first level even got a new glass floor, giving visitors a thrilling view straight down!

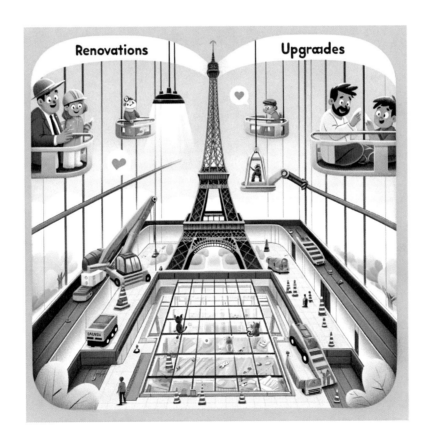

The Eiffel Tower keeps standing tall and strong, like a superhero of the city. It's a reminder to all of us that people can create beautiful things and overcome tough challenges. Just like the tower has lasted through storms and sunny days, it shows us that we can be brave and keep going, no matter what. The Eiffel Tower is like a big, iron cheerleader, cheering us on to be our best and never give up!

Visit our author page for more children's books,
and remember to follow us for updates on new releases,
including illustrated storybooks, fun-fact picture books,
coloring books, activity books for kids, and more:

Amazon.com/author/88

Nicole Damon

√ Following   HOME   ABOUT   ALL BOOKS

Quick look

Easter Golden Egg Adventure: A Story of...

Kindle Edition

$0⁰⁰ kindleunlimited

Other formats: Paperback

Quick look

Forest Kingdom: A Story About the...

Kindle Edition

$0⁰⁰ kindleunlimited

or **$2.99** to buy

Quick look

Temples, Beaches, Nature and More

Kindle Edition

$0⁰⁰ kindleunlimited

or **$2.99** to buy

Other formats: Paperback

Quick look

Gate Bridge and Beyond: Discovering the...

⭐ 1

Kindle Edition

$0⁰⁰ kindleunlimited

or **$2.99** to buy

Other formats: Paperback

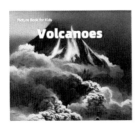

Made in the USA
Las Vegas, NV
03 May 2024